The Power of Not Caring

How To Regain Control When We Are Constantly Worrying About What Others Think Of Us

Grace Scott

Table of Contents

Introduction

It is important to understand why we care about what people think. The part of our mind that produces this fear is often in place to protect us. For example, if we don't care what others think then we might go out and murder everyone we hate or run through shopping malls completely naked.

The real reason why we care what people think is because we base our identity on everyone's judgments of us. It doesn't matter whether the judgment is positive or negative. Because we think that part of our identity is how people view us, then we must protect that so our identity is not affected.

Lao Tzu once wrote, "Care about people's approval and you will be their prisoner."

At one point or another, we allow ourselves to become prisoners. We define our own limitations by thinking too much about people's perception of us. However, we simply cannot judge ourselves from the eyes of others.

Although it is true enough that there are some useful things you can pick up by listening to other people's feedback, thinking about these things too much may also become destructive. When you care too much, you will end up living your life in limbo. And that is nowhere near true living.

Caring too much about what others think, whether or not you realize it, is not helpful for your growth as a human being. You must care, but never to the point of sacrificing your own happiness just to get the approval of others. Ultimately, you should be in control of your own life. Do not let others dictate your path.

Why exactly do people care too much?

One of the main reasons is that we are afraid of being rejected. We cringe at the thought of disapproval. We ultimately want to belong and that makes us feel much better about ourselves. Another reason why we care too much is that we simply want to be viewed as important. This is why we seek positive attention, so we can be perceived as "normal" in society.

When does caring become problematic?

It is perfectly all right to consider other people's opinions, but to live by them is plain wrong. A lot of people live their lives unhappily. They limit their lives and restrict their choices only to those that other people approve of. They live in the shadow of other people's expectations, and end up not living their life at all.

Just be yourself.

This must be one of the most overused pieces of advice ever, but it does not make it any less true. Everything starts from within. Learn to accept yourself and others will follow, at least those who are worthy of being in your life.

It is very important that you get to know yourself first. Be your own person. Do not submit to other people's opinions. Do not surrender yourself to their expectations. Meet your own standards and values, not theirs. Live on your own terms. Prioritize your goals. Use other people's feedback as a point of reassessment.

Life is not a popularity contest. Some people will like you while others will hate you for no reason at all. You cannot change that. However, you can change your life. You can choose to create your own destiny.

If you feel like you have been unhappy for a while, there may be something wrong with the way you are living your life. It is normal to be unsatisfied once in a while, but never always. If this is the case, it may be time to start asking who you are really living your life for. Are you living for your own purpose?

Chapter 1: Who Are You Living For?

Shake it off all you want, but it seems too difficult to simply stop caring about what other people think of us. We are social beings and it is only natural to consider other people in our lives, but when does it become too much?

Admit it or not, you care about what others think of you. People who declare they don't are more than likely just being pretentious. You cannot stop caring; it is in your nature. Yet it is absolutely wrong to live your life for others, to make your decisions based on other people's perceptions and expectations.

Are you caught in your parent's expectations?

John fell in love with art when he was old enough to scribble, but he belongs to a family of lawyers. Since the day he was born, his destiny has already been decided. He will be a lawyer like his brothers, his sister, his father, his grandfather, his uncles and the rest of his family. Although he wanted to study art and make art, he kept it to himself and decided to follow his parent's expectations of him.

It is quite typical for parents to want the best for their children. This is why they always try to influence their children's decisions in a genuine effort to keep them on the right track. It can be smothering, but they only want what is best for their kids. The question is: Are you one of those kids?

What role do your parents have to play in your choice of college? Are you pursuing good education based on their standards? Is it your dream you are chasing after, or is it theirs? While you may not want to disappoint your parents, you do have to stand up for yourself at some point. At the end of the day, you will be living your own life, but are you willing to live it on their terms? Can you bear the thought of letting go of your dreams to pursue what they dream that you will become someday? Pleasing your parents is one thing, but living only to please them is wrong.

Are you making choices because of peer pressure?

Paul always hangs out with his buddies and he enjoys their company quite a lot, but as they grow older his friend's interests start to change. Paul is interested in girls too, but he is simply not quite there yet. He does not feel ready to be with a girl and there is no one in particular that interests him in their school. All of Paul's friends have a girl of their own now. He is the only one left in the group without one. Afraid that he will be labeled a loser, he randomly picks a girl to call his girlfriend.

Fitting in with a group of friends can feel absolutely wonderful. The sense of belonging can put more meaning in your life. It simply makes things more fun when you share it with other people outside your family. But there are times too, when you may be forced to do something just because you are afraid of falling out of the loop.

Young boys and girls especially chase after the opposite sex. When all their friends are with a significant other, they also feel the need to be with someone. They want to be able to relate to their friends. Ultimately, they want to be accepted. In this sense, having a boyfriend or girlfriend can seem like a competition. Just because your friends are in a relationship, you also feel the need to find or be in one, and this is not only true for young adults. It haunts even people of age, especially single individuals surrounded by friends who are in coupledom.

Who are you dressing up for?

Lizzie is in high school and she is quite lucky to hang out with the popular kids. All her friends wear the latest fashion trends, they shop every weekend and they only buy clothes from expensive boutiques. Although she may feel it is ridiculous to spend that much money on a dress, she does anyway. She simply wants to fit in, and she pays the price for popularity.

Fashion is an interesting subject matter. But when you put on clothes, whose style are you really wearing? Are you trying to express yourself or are you simply trying to make an impression? People should always make an effort to look presentable, but there is something wrong when you copy someone else's style and don't follow your own. When you shop, do you really want to go after designer and rather expensive clothing? Are you looking at the style rather than the price tag? When you wear your clothes, are you doing it to show off?

Are you a class clown?

Rob's parents are divorced. His dad, whom he is staying with, does not have a job and has a drinking problem. He does not want his friends from school to find out how pathetic his life is, so he tries to project a different image, far from the real one.

A positive disposition in life is encouraged, but people also say that the saddest people are the clowns. They always have a smile on their face but in reality, they only put on that smile in an effort to please others, to make other people happy and hide their own sadness.

Do you want to get fit for the sake of health or for some other reason?

Mary is not exactly obese but she is on the heavy side compared to her girlfriends who are just skin and bones. She feels she looks fat. She does not like her curves so she decides to save up enough money to undergo liposuction during the summer.

The call for health has become louder and louder. It seems that people are now much more conscious about their body. But when you diet, when you go to the gym or buy expensive products, or go through expensive treatments, are you doing it for yourself or are you simply worried about your body image?

Why do you want to lose weight? Is it because you are afraid of being called fat? Is it because all your friends are skinny? What's stopping you from leaving an abusive relationship?

Why can you not quit your job? Why is it too difficult to move out of your comfort zone?

A Sense of Belonging Makes Us Feel Comfortable.

Somehow, being in a group, being accepted by family, relatives, friends, colleagues and even strangers is what most people live for even without realizing it. It feels much more comfortable not to go through rejection. But only aiming to be accepted cannot make you feel truly happy. It can only help you avoid fear and rejection.

Chapter 2: Are You a Lost Soul?

Studies indicate that people can benefit from what others think. That's because other people can see things in you which you may not be aware of. In this way, it is also helpful to acknowledge other people's opinion of you. However, everything should have a limit.

What is caring too much?

How can you tell if someone or some people are pulling your strings? It does not necessarily mean they command you to do things you may not exactly agree with. Sometimes or most of the time, we allow people around us to pull our strings. That said, below are the top 6 signs that you run the risk of getting lost; hints to warn you when you are caring way too much.

You are always concerned about what others may think or say about you.

You hesitate to share your good ideas when you are in a group.

You always feel the need to seek approval from others first.

You are afraid to speak up.

You hesitate to express an unpopular opinion.

You have spent so much money on clothes, jewelry, cars, houses and other material possessions because you think what or how much you own defines your worth.

What happens when you care too much?

The bottom line is it will not do you any good to constantly think about what others may say or think, because you will only lose yourself and your real purpose.

Other people's opinions take the center stage in your life.

A wise man will tell you that only you can define yourself. You can choose your destiny and you can make your own situation. What if you get to decide on your life but the things you choose are those that conform to other people's opinion of you? Are you truly free?

When you become too concerned with what the rest of the world say about you, it is a sure sign of insecurity. People develop their opinions based on complex variables. They may be able to see some aspects of your personality and values, but the plain truth is that they also have their own prejudices. Such prejudices inadvertently affect their perception of you.

In other words, it will not help if you focus on other people's opinions. In fact, it can be very problematic. For one, you pay a lot of attention and spend too much energy on things you cannot truly control - the way others think. Two, you are taking the focus away from what you can actually control - yourself.

You should be able to accept the fact that it is impossible to please everyone. If you want to be accepted for who you are, you should stop conforming to their expectations or trying to change their perceptions. Rather, you should be more authentic. You should stay true to yourself.

You are a yes man.

There is a movie by Jim Carrey about being a yes man. In some situations, saying yes can be very helpful, but you must also learn the importance of saying no.

If you are terrified of the world, of disappointing your peers, then you are in deep trouble. Do not agree or say yes just because you think the other person may take it the wrong way. You do not have to say yes just to demonstrate your manners. An insincere yes is actually more disappointing than a genuine no.

You have to be in the spotlight, always!

People like talking about themselves. They like to tell other people their accomplishments, where they have been, and where they are headed to. If you think it is a sign of confidence, you are wrong. People who become too boastful are rather insecure. People who overdo it are constantly seeking validation. They do what they do because somehow, it makes them feel better about themselves. It is the only way they know how to impress those around them, or at least those who are willing to or pretend to listen.

By lifting themselves high, they tend to make other people feel inferior. If you are crossing this border, you have more problems than you may be willing to admit.

You tend to do everything to gain favor.

Not everyone will like you. Every one of us probably has our own share of haters. That is a fact of life. Do not play nice, pretend to be happy, polite or what have you just to change other people's perception of you. There will always be people with whom you will not jive. This does not mean there is something wrong with you. It is probably just a personality conflict.

Not everything can be fixed. It will be a huge waste of your time and energy to try to fix things that you simply have no power over.

Your decisions are based on other people's expectations.

It may not seem problematic when you decided to go and get a degree that your parents wanted you to take. But in the long run, you will realize how much of a problem it can be. Small choices have ended up ruining so many lives. You may not realize it now but you will soon when you start feeling miserable.

Some people just seem to exist, and they never live the way others do. What they are lacking is passion. If you feel unhappy about your situation, you probably paid too much attention to meeting other people's expectations of you.

You have to create the life you actually want to live. Listen to what your heart tells you. Pursue your dreams even if they do not exactly match up to what your parents, friends, colleagues or everybody else expect. Do not put yourself in a box and allow yourself to become a prisoner of other people's hopes for you.

What would you become?

When you allow yourself to be controlled by other people's opinions and expectations, you will never be truly happy. Sure, you may feel good every now and then by getting a tap on the shoulder for a job well done, but living your life should not feel like a job, something that you do only because you feel you have to.

When you care too much, you lose your own identity. You lose the meaning of life. You cannot live life fulfilling the purpose of others. One day, you will wake up wondering where ten or twenty years have gone and regret how you spent them trying to please the people around you.

Chapter 3: Why Do I Care?

It may not be possible to completely stop the constant worrying about what other people think or say about you, but there are ways to keep it within a healthy amount. Quit obsessing about other's opinions, or else you will find yourself lost in a negative cycle.

When caring hurts more than it helps you, it must stop. Steer yourself to the right direction, and turn your life around by following this advice.

Quit over-thinking.

You are not the center of the universe. Your loved ones may treat you like you are the most important person in the world, but not everyone shares the same opinion. Not everyone will take the time to scrutinize your personality and analyze your flaws. They probably have other and more important things to do than to be a judge in your life.

If you still do not believe it, you are encouraged to put it to the test. Try to make a change in yourself. It could be anything physical that is out of the ordinary. Now, check people's reactions. Your family, friends and other people you spend the most time with will probably notice the change, and are likely to share some comments too. However, it is very unlikely that a complete stranger will care.

When you start the pattern of over-thinking, stop yourself immediately. To counter attack the negative cycle, recognize the positive aspects of your life or your personality. This practice can at least help boost your damaged self-esteem.

Finding the right perspective.

Are you paying too much attention to the details and end up completely missing the big picture? That is exactly what you do when you care too much, and this makes life more stressful than enjoyable. Instead, try to put things in proper perspective.

Life is too short to spend time worrying about nonsense. You simply cannot have everything you want, and you definitely cannot have everyone's approval. Instead of focusing on what we don't have, we should be focusing on what we already have and be thankful for it, because gratitude is the real way to happiness.

You can also make a list of the things that you are thankful for. This list becomes tangible proof that things are in the right place. Also, it will show you that your life is not as bad after all. Appreciate all the things that life throws at you, because what matters the most is living your life with your own purpose, not other people's.

Building confidence.

Quit second guessing yourself. While you do need to make sure that your decisions are well thought out, you also need to find a way to build your confidence. This will make you more comfortable about your decisions and actions.

When you feel too conscious about something, people can sense that. Take for instance, someone who is wearing something outrageous, like a hat too big for their head. People will probably turn their heads away. They may even giggle or whisper to one another. But if that person wearing a big hat does not seem to care, eventually the people around the person will stop caring too.

Everyone is insecure. And some people are just vultures waiting for someone who has much less self-confidence to take down. That is when you are more likely to be attacked. But if you have confidence they will sense it, and that can make you almost untouchable.

So how exactly do you build your confidence? Try smiling more often. As the saying goes, smile and the rest of the world will smile with you. Adopt a more positive outlook in life. Instead of anticipating failure, visualize your success. Finally, break down your life goals into smaller ones. Take one step at a time. And do not forget to celebrate your accomplishments, no matter how small or minor they may seem to be.

Take control of your emotions.

Mixed emotions can put you through a roller coaster ride that will make you feel nauseous and overwhelmed. A simple solution for taking control is to separate yourself from the emotion. Recognize what you are feeling and observe it. The mere act of putting the emotion under observation can help separate you from it. That can also make the emotion fade into thin air.

Accept yourself for who you really are.

How can you expect to have other people's approval when you do not approve of yourself in the first place? To save yourself from the limbo of negative emotions, constant fear and worrying, you must first learn to accept yourself for who you are.

Make a list of all the things you do not like about yourself. Separate the things you can change and those you do not have control over. Change for the better, but do not even attempt to make impossible changes in yourself, as you will only end up more frustrated. You will soon realize that you have been worrying about unimportant things and it has been a complete waste of energy and time.

Enjoy your individuality.

You are unique, and you should celebrate your uniqueness. There is nothing more boring than being ordinary or being like everyone else. Sure, you may have some flaws, but these are all part of your individuality - so accept and celebrate it.

Imagine a worry-free life.

It may be a little more challenging to see the light at the end of the tunnel when you feel like your life is in a rut, but it may help to think the other way. Imagine what kind of life you will have if you are not constantly worrying about what others are thinking.

Imagine getting rid of the burden of your fear of rejection. You will find yourself free from expectations. Don't you want that kind of life? Imagine all the things you could do if you do not care too much about opinions and expectations. You could be unstoppable!

Other people worry as well.

The funny thing is that other people may have the same concerns as you do. They spend 90 percent of their time worrying about what they are doing or what they are wearing, and if other people think that they look ridiculous. That means they have less time to spend criticizing you. Now though, it is time you leave that boat and steer your own ship.

Respect yourself.

Do not allow other people to trample on you or take you for granted. Recognize your worth as an individual and do not let others treat you as less of a human being.

Surround yourself with positive people.

Negative people will drag you down no matter what. They suck your energy and motivation away. Avoid these kinds of people. If they are putting you through a great deal of stress, then it is a good sign to block them. Instead, surround yourself with positive energy. Be with positive people. The energy can be contagious.

Stop being submissive

Take pride on who you are as a human being. Do not follow others blindly. Question if you must. Stop being a pushover. Stand up for yourself. Show them you are not the type of person that can be pushed around and treated like an inferior human being.

Be yourself

There are many things you can probably change about yourself for the better, but do not change just because other people tell you to. When you start a change, make sure you are doing it for yourself, and not for other people.

Never be afraid of your own true colors. You are beautiful in your own way. You are absolutely good enough!

Decide firmly.

Taking back control over your life starts with making a conscious decision. You have to stop caring too much about other people's opinions. You do not have to be mean. You do not have to compromise your values and beliefs.

You can be yourself without being offensive. Try and stop caring about getting other people's approval and worrying about not fitting in. There is no one else like you and that is a blessing. Be yourself. This can be the best contribution to the world.

Chapter 4: In the Real World

One of the greatest obstacles to your success is probably your approval-seeking behavior. When you try to control other people's way of thinking, you would most likely end up being controlled by fear. Here is a list of many great reasons why you should stop caring too much about others opinions.

Not everyone will like you.

People will always have bad things to say about others. It is just a reflection of their insecurities. You cannot make them change, but you can change your perception by stopping the habit of caring too much.

You do not need their "approval" in order to be happy.

Their approval is not a prerequisite to your happiness; so do not allow them to define your worth as a person. You are good enough regardless of what they think or say about you.

People will think about whatever they want to think about.

There is no way to control other people's thoughts. They will keep thinking what they want to think about. As mentioned in the earlier chapter of this book, everyone has their own prejudices that affects their judgment. It is not something you can control.

Seeking approval is a waste of time and energy.

If you cannot change the way people think, then why spend your time and energy trying? It simply does not make any sense. Imagine the things you can accomplish if you can spend your time and energy on more productive activities.

Take control of your own life.

If you feel like someone else is holding the string and you are the puppet. It came to be that way, because you allowed it to be. You impose these limitations and restrictions on yourself by caring too much about other people's opinions and expectations, but you should be controlling your life. You should make the decisions that suit you. Otherwise, you will ultimately suffer from unhappiness just trying to please others.

Your approval is what is most important.

Some people may genuinely like you. Others may absolutely hate you. And some could not care less.

When you learn to accept yourself for who you are, it becomes less important of what others may think of you. If you are confident about who you are as a person, you will be happier. At the end of the day, what matters the most is to understand the value of self acceptance, and living a happy and fulfilling life.

Nobody is perfect. Everyone makes mistakes. There are things that are totally out of your control including how other people react about you. Accept this as a fact and you will learn to be more self-forgiving and more self-accepting.

Conclusion

We are social beings and it is quite normal for us to consider other people's opinions. In fact, in some ways, this can be helpful to our growth, but anything in excess can be hurtful rather than helpful. So, what must you do?

Pay attention and stop worrying.

Nothing good comes from worrying too much. You will only suffer from anxiety and become trapped in an unhappy life. Realize the fact you are your worst critic. Do not read too much on things or take comments too seriously.

Pick only those that matter.

You know you are in trouble when you care too much about a complete stranger's opinions. Know whose opinions matter the most in your life, but even then, draw limitations.

Utilize feedback.

Just because someone gives you a negative feedback does not mean they do not like you in a personal level. You may be able to use the feedback for improvement. When you receive one, ask yourself whether or not it will help you improve if you apply it in your personal life.

You may find yourself torn between considering what makes you happy and what makes the important people in your life happy. People who truly care about you will not be concerned whether or not you take their advice. Their main concern is your happiness and self fulfillment.

Sure, your parents may be a little disappointed when you do not go to the college that they picked out. They only want the best for you, but they will certainly understand the fact that you want to fulfill your own dreams.

Set your own goals. Never let anyone do it for you.

Don't forget to protect your values. Consult your values when something does not feel or seem right. Have conviction, and people will respect you.

Remember, Life is not about being popular. Free yourself from that kind of mentality. Do not be afraid to fight for things you want even when no one is supporting you.

If you want to set yourself free and be happy, know who you are and know where you are going. You can only live your life to the fullest when you fulfill your own purpose. Being considerate about other people is a good trait, but know your boundaries. It is your life. After all, you are now free to choose on how you live it.

Thank you for reading "The Power of Not Caring". If you enjoyed this book. Please take the time to share your thoughts and post a review on Amazon. It'd be greatly appreciated.

Thank you and good luck!

Grace Scott

Made in the USA
Lexington, KY
18 December 2019